The
ATTITUDE
CONNECTION

Focus On
Quality

by
JOE BLACK

Foreword by
J. Patrick Danahy

LVB
LIFE VISION BOOKS
P.O. BOX 98, CAMPOBELLO, SC 29322
(803) 468-4749

First printing 1991
Second printing 1992
Third printing 1993
Fourth printing 1995

ISBN 0-9628474-2-9

LCCN 90-092235

ATTENTION CORPORATIONS, COLLEGES, UNIVERSITIES, AND PROFESSIONAL ORGANIZATIONS: Quantity discounts are available on bulk purchases of this book for educational purposes, gifts, or fund raising. Special books or book excerpts can also be created to fit specific needs. For information, please contact our Special Sales Department, Life Vision Books, P.O. Box 98, Campobello, SC 29322, or call (803) 468-4749.

Here's What People are Saying . . .

"My whole philosophy is based upon possessing and maintaining the proper attitude. If you feel this way also, you will find Joe Black's book helpful, motivating, enjoyable, and invaluable."

> Lou Holtz
> Head Football Coach
> University of Notre Dame

"The *people* side to quality is the one that is most neglected, but is most important. I've had my son and daughter read it also. You are right on!"

> Dr. Norvin Clontz, President
> Greige Fine Goods &
> Chemical Division
> Milliken & Company

"*The Attitude Connection* is a great short book to give to your associates and an excellent guide to managing by values."

> Charles Eitel, President
> Collins & Aikman Corporation

"The Attitude Connection–Focus On Quality has meant quite a bit to Warren Featherbone. You have a unique ability to help people rediscover the great truths in life. Your vignettes are a joy to read, and they convey simple yet very powerful principles. Thank you for sharing them with us."

> Charles E. Whalen, Jr.
> President & Chief Executive Officer
> The Warren Featherbone Company

"I found it to be concise, witty and more importantly, practical to the point of immediate utilization. I will pass it on to all those who work with me at Kings Computers."

> John Russell Osburn
> President
> King's Business Machines

"It is entertaining, thought provoking and poignant. Your commitment to quality and excellence on both an individual and group level comes through loud and clear."

> Dr. B. Rhett Meyers
> Medical Director
> Marshall Pickens Hospital

"I enjoyed your approach to simplify our idea of quality. For some reason we associate a complication to quality–very difficult to define–requires everyday scrutiny, etc. But in your book as you compared quality to work and life, it seems somehow to clear things up."

> Stan W. Vinson
> Vice President Manufacturing
> West Point Pepperell

"The Attitude Connection proves that it isn't necessary to have a volume in order to present a powerful message. It is a thought provoking book."

Jules Lasnick
Executive Vice President
Springs Industries

"I do not have a big appetite for management books, but yours I found to be so readable that I read it in one sitting. It's full of good sense and reminders."

C. John Billings
Director of Management Services
Courtaulds

"I read *The Attitude Connection* cover to cover and thoroughly enjoyed it. It certainly applies to lawyers and law firms as well as business people."

J. Steve Warren
Attorney–Labor & Employment Law
Jackson, Lewis, Schnitzler, & Krupman

"Makes for easy reading and thought provoking moments. I'm having my staff get copies of the book."

Sherry Len Turner
Vice President–Human Resources
Frito-Lay, Inc,

Dedication

In memory of Wellons Jervey whose smile, infectious enthusiasm, and courage touched forever everyone who knew her.

Acknowledgments

I wish to say a special thank you to the following: my wife Kathy, for all the reasons she knows, my aunt Joanne Alexander, for her proofreading and editing, my aunt Julia Alexander, for always encouraging me toward excellence, and my longtime friend, Jim Rutledge, who encouraged me to go into business for myself.

I also wish to thank my partner Pudge Tate, for his continuous support and encouragement. Thanks also to my team members at Executive Quality Management: Jan Hill, Lisa Neal, Juanita White, Darryl Thompson, David Black, Fred Hardee, Bill Stoddard, Lewis Rollins, Steve Carter, Rick Gully, Ken Spires, Bill Robinson, Paul Edel, Charlie Schinck, Travis Bruce, Becky Ehrenstein, and Nikki Corson.

And thank you, Pamela Rattray Brown McCulley, for the illustrations in this book.

Table of Contents

Foreword

Joe Black is a "carrier" of a positive attitude. If you spend much time around him or read this book, you are bound to catch some of his infectious attitude.

I first met Joe Black four years ago when we decided our company might benefit from a Quality Improvement Process. We interviewed EQM, of which Joe is co-founder and co-chairman, as a potential consultant partner. He sold us on his approach for our division, including the foundation of an attitude change throughout our unit.

The Attitude Connection contains many of the stories and examples he used to "sell" us and to actually bring about an attitude change that led to tremendous improvement. We used to tease Joe about "overselling" his product. In four years, he has never stopped living the pearls of insight one finds strewn throughout the book.

The Attitude Connection is a collection of experiences, stories, and parables that conveys ideas and principles for personal and professional living. Both in person and in the book, Joe Black uses humor (including laughing at himself) to open lines of communication. Quotations relating to the issue in each parable are provided and there is an opportunity for the reader to record his or her thoughts or reactions. Within these covers, you will come face to face with the reality that any leader must live what he or she professes before they can have a continuing impact on others to change.

The *power* of and *human need* for recognition and individual dignity are illustrated in many of Joe Black's true experiences. *The Attitude Connection* is a network or matrix, weaving together a web of philosophy for professional and personal life. It is not structured, but easily read, providing many points of focus for whatever strikes your fancy.

Today, businesses in the United States face a crisis. Throughout our history, we have had the natural resources, finances, and markets to operate our own isolated economy. This is now being threatened by foreign competitors, who, without all the basic resources, have harnessed their human potential out of necessity. They are now claiming US markets with a focus on defining and meeting customer specifications.

Our challenge is to harness the tremendous potential within the human resources of our own culture and meet this competition in a global marketplace. *The Attitude Connection* provides insight into the first step in realizing our professional and personal potential. It truly provides many keys to changing our attitudes and unlocking the human potential within each of us.

Joe Black is an excellent communicator. He is able to reach out and connect with people across our entire social spectrum, and he practices what he preaches. *The Attitude Connection* has a similar effect. This book will touch everyone–read it and implement the parables that turn you on.

J. Patrick Danahy
CEO, Cone Mills Corporation

Preface

After graduating from college, I was fortunate to find my way into America's textile industry. Little did I realize two decades ago what a tremendous foundation this field would afford me in manufacturing, human resources, training, public affairs, college relations, and quality management.

I first became involved in total quality management in 1980 while working for Milliken & Company in Spartanburg, South Carolina. Prior to forming my own company, I had the privilege of serving as quality facilitator for Milliken's largest division.

In 1985, it became clear that my focus in life should be to share with others the great value a total quality mentality can add to one's personal and professional life. Along with two partners, I formed Executive Quality Management, Inc., (EQM) as a vehicle for custom designing quality processes for large and small firms. Now we serve organizations all over the United States as well as England and Canada. We provide curb service. When they blow their horns, we come. These companies tell us they've never had less than a three-to-one payback in the first 12 months.

Giving the knowledge is the easy part–implementation is tough. That's where we shine, and so can you. The concepts in this book come from my experiences with many customers over the past 10 years. You can achieve the results you want by building quality personal and professional relationships. That foundation is part of what we share with our clients, and those techniques are interwoven throughout these pages.

In any quality improvement process, look for long-term results. Think of quality management as a resource to *support* what you're after. Most good companies want to do what's right concerning quality. They want to grow and nurture their people. I've been fortunate to work with good companies who want to become even better. The key is continually improving quality and customer service. That's what gives a company the personal touch.

In writing this book, I've shared some key insights into what makes excellent companies–the best of the best–tick. Here in these pages, you, too, can find the creativity and innovation to approach your work and home anew. *The Attitude Connection* can change your perspective of what Quality is all about.

Introduction

Most of the reflections shared here are simply observations or reactions to everyday events in my life and work. One of my great joys has been the opportunity to make new friends and acquaintances and build on old relationships as well. It's a great gift all of us can share and benefit from.

Had it not been for others, I would have enjoyed no experiences to share with you. I'm not a "do-it-yourself" writer; I'm a "do-it-with-help" writer, for without people to interact with and learn from, I would have little to write about.

My hope is you'll read something in this book you can relate to, which may in turn encourage you, help you, or open your mind for future plans. I hope you'll come to realize more clearly than ever before that you can and indeed do make a difference.

Joe Black

prbm

1

Attitudes Are Contagious

Most people let outside forces affect their attitudes. It's hard not to in this fast-paced world. Your clock radio awakens you in the morning with the news—it's seldom good. You turn on your television and hear the world news. Then you drive to work, or take the bus or train—and get the news again! Stop and think about it. In addition to coping with the children, your spouse, and the dog at the start of each work day, you are bombarded with bad news!

You may ask, "How in the world can I be expected to have a cheerful, can-do, positive attitude with all the added problems at work?" Well, the good news is you *can* have a positive attitude! Millions of people facing similar or worse problems than you and I face every day manage to keep a positive outlook on life.

How do they do it? It's really fairly simple. Have you ever stopped to realize that each of us has the same decision to make each day—a decision we can make before we even get out of bed? Resolve this early: "Am I going to respond positively or negatively to the realities I will face today?"

Know right then you're going to respond to those realities with a positive attitude. Most of us can't change the realities of our lives. We can only decide how we're going to respond to them. It's always within our power to choose the positive response. Having a positive attitude doesn't mean you're always on top of the world. You can even cry and still respond positively to a difficult situation.

Medical science continues to compile hard data suggesting your outlook on life and a positive attitude can add years to your life. More importantly, a positive attitude allows you to enjoy the wonderful gift of life every day with your family, friends, and work associates.

Think about it. The winner will be you and everyone you come in contact with. Attitudes are contagious; are yours worth catching?

JUST NOTES

_____

_____

_____

_____

_____

_____

"An attitude is more powerful than any circumstance."

Unknown

_____

_____

_____

_____

_____

_____

_____

_____

_____

_____

_____

_____

_____

_____

2

Quality, the Big "Q"

What does quality mean to you? Responses to this question often vary greatly within the same company. Many people see quality as a product, meeting specifications, doing their best, and so on. Having excellent teams in business requires that we define quality and understand it.

At Executive Quality Management, Inc., we think of quality as being much more than merely a functional product or service. *Quality Is Everything We Do*. It affects both our personal and professional lives. How we answer the telephone, how we deal with others, whether we deliver the correct product or service on time–all these things and more are what quality is all about. People have been taught to think of quality in terms of products or services offered to a customer. Most businesspeople talk a good fight about their quality processes, but their behavior on the job often doesn't truly reflect a serious commitment to quality.

If companies focus on the "Big Q" (where quality is everything you do) rather than the "little q" (quality is a product or service), a culture change will likely take place. We'll define culture as how we do things around here. This requires all members of the team to rethink how they run their jobs. It means changing our behavior in how we approach our jobs and live our lives. A total Big Q mentality encourages new ideas and attitudes and determines how we go about solving problems.

The Big Q approach to quality is not just using one tool. For instance, it's not just total employee involvement programs or mere statistical quality control. The Big Q is a flexible, evolutionary process requiring the very best of each member of the team.

Often companies get trapped into thinking one tool is the answer, and many quality gurus would have employers believe that, too. Just as a doctor would never prescribe the same medication to every one of his patients, no one quality tool should be prescribed for every company. Each company has different hurts, wants, and needs, and the quality process should be molded to fit those unique requirements.

Each person in an organization must continually have his Big Q awareness raised. This requires that top management understand investing in the growth and development of their people is as necessary as investing in hardware, software, and machinery. Regardless of how you cut it, it always comes back to people.

Recently, I watched a television commercial stressing the reliability and excellence of a particular Japanese automobile, for example. A few minutes after the commercial, I picked up a magazine and saw an advertisement by a US auto maker stressing what a nice guy Mr. Goodwrench is. In other words, the car made in the United States is not going to work and you'll have to go meet this fictitious service man at your local car dealership.

There is a world of difference between the Big Q and the little q mentality. In the United States, we must embrace and implement the Big Q mentality if we are to recapture our lost markets and remain competitive in the world marketplace.

JUST NOTES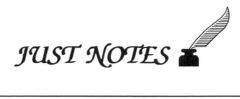

"Here is the simple but powerful rule...always give people more than they expect to get."

Nelson Boswell

3

Fire at 102 Shady Lane

On my fortieth birthday, I was working with a company in Mississippi. A group of 25 managers and administrative associates had gathered in the small town's fire station for their quality seminar. That setting actually worked out very well, for most of us were kids at heart. Being in the fire station was still exciting to us.

During the seminar, a participant responsible for all training in the company approached me at the break. He began to explain to me how much there was to be done. After listening carefully to him, I concluded that this person was not likely to make it on his new job without focusing on the vital few problems instead of the trivial many.

Then it came to me. The answer to this man's problems was right under our noses—the fire house! I asked that man to pretend he was a firefighter and had just received a call to go to 102 Shady Lane to put out a house fire.

"What would you do?" I asked him.

He thought for a moment and said, "I'd rally my troops, get on the fire engine, go directly to the fire, and put it out!"

I replied, "Exactly! You get an A+." Then I continued, "If on the way to 102 Shady Lane, you saw other houses on fire, what would you do?"

Looking a little puzzled, he thought a minute and said, "I'd radio back to the firehouse to send more trucks and manpower to those houses."

"Fantastic!" I said, "You get another A+." By then, he was really into the conversation without knowing where it was leading him.

Then I rang his fire bell. "You, sir, must put out one fire at a time. You will always pass other houses on fire as you head to your target of 102 Shady Lane. You may want to stop and try to put out every fire, but you can't do it. It's simply impossible. You must identify which house you *are* going to save and drive quickly and directly to it to extinguish the blaze."

I continued, "Yes, you're right about the other fires; after you radio for more trucks and manpower, you trust your team to take care of them. But you stay on your course and remain focused on the immediate problem."

To put it another way, it's better to plant one tree in a scorched forest than to worry and talk about replanting the entire forest. The moral is to do something–stop just talking about it. *Do* something. In today's companies, we desperately need proactive leaders, people who not only talk but who also do concrete things.

This gentleman and I have since become close friends. He has left that company and now heads the training/education program for another large firm. He's also become an expert at identifying fires and putting them out, and has become even better at fire prevention.

Don't let the fires you see every day on your job blind you to your objectives. Steer your engine to 102 Shady Lane and put that sucker out! You'll sleep better and worry less.

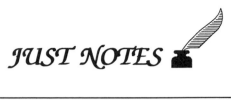

JUST NOTES

"Nothing can add more power to your life than concentrating all of your energies on a limited set of targets."

Nido Qubein

4

Are You a Squirter?

Has anyone ever squirted you with cold water? If so, chances are it wasn't an enjoyable experience, especially if it was a surprise. Many people go through life "squirting" others. They don't carry water guns or hoses, but instead arm themselves with bad attitudes and all forms of negative trash they will hose you down with in a New York minute!

We all know people who just love to squirt. They're usually an unhappy lot who seem to enjoy being critical of others. If you ask squirters how they feel, they'll share all kinds of unpleasantness for at least half an hour.

Squirters aren't bad people; they simply have never understood there is a better way to live. They refuse to believe that being positive beats preaching and practicing doom and gloom.

None of us can escape squirters. They're everywhere. They squirt others with negative words and phrases: "No," "But," "Nothing is going to change around here," "We've always done it this way," "I feel so bad," "We can't be the best," "We tried that and it didn't work," etc. Instead of adding value, squirters add only ruin. Can you change a squirter? Probably not;

however, you can set a positive example and hope the squirter will recognize negative behavior and choose to change it.

Don't confuse squirting with telling it like it is. You can be honest and still approve or improve a given situation. If you choose to be a leader, expect to stay wet. Squirters will hose you down every day. I know one executive whose desk displays this sign, "No squirting allowed on second floor." You guessed it—his office is on the second floor!

Are you a squirter? If so, consider the damage you inflict on yourself and those around you. There's no place for squirters in an excellent company.

JUST NOTES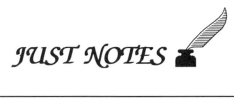

_____

_____

_____

_____

_____

_____

"As a rule, those who complain about the way the ball bounces are usually the ones who dropped it."

Bernard Meltzer

_____

_____

_____

_____

_____

_____

_____

_____

_____

_____

_____

_____

_____

5

You Can Add Value or Ruin

There he was, running around his department, cursing and hollering and scaring his people half to death. This manager had been wronged by a corporate decision which affected his relationship with his major customer. The plant hadn't been notified of a change in specifications regarding a large order, which had already gone out to the customer. The customer had called to say he was shipping the order back to the manager, and the manager knew he'd probably be blamed for the error. Does all this sound familiar?

I happened upon my disgruntled friend. After a major squirt or two from him, I offered to buy him a cup of coffee. He agreed, and we went to the canteen where he continued to rant and rave. By this time, he had really worked himself into a stew. Everyone was scared even to come close to him. After 30 minutes or so, he asked, "Well, wouldn't you be ready to kill the SOB if he had given you the wrong specs? Wouldn't you feel the same way I do? Say something."

I replied, "Yes, I'd be very upset as well." As my reply sank in, I watched his veins reduce in size and his red face fade to a sunset pink. Then I asked, " What are your plans to prevent this from happening again?" He hadn't yet begun to address this question. He looked at me and said, "I'm going to call the guy and tell him never to set foot in my plant again!"

I then asked permission for another question. Permission granted, I said, "Have you considered documenting the cost of this error to your company? Then based on clear and accurate data, you can request a team be formed to prevent it from happening again." To my amazement, he said, "You know, that's a good idea." After further discussion, he finally smiled as he realized what was happening.

- The error had been made
- The error was serious, but not intentional
- He had reacted very poorly

He now had a choice:
  A. Continue the status quo and add ruin to himself and to those around him.
  B. Take positive corrective action, swallow some pride, and suggest a team be formed between his plant and the corporate office to insure errors of this type don't occur again.

So often, indeed most of the time, I find managers choose A over B. It takes courage to control emotions and set a positive example for others to follow—to sit down with people you may dislike and work to make improvements. This manager focused on getting back at an individual instead of preventing the problem from happening again.

We all face similar situations at work. The choice is always ours to make. Are we going to add value or ruin? Do we think, "get even" or "prevent this from happening again"? The happiest and most successful people I know choose the latter. The choice is ours.

JUST NOTES

_____

_____

_____

_____

_____

_____

"I can't change the direction of the wind, but I can adjust my sails to always reach my destination."

Jimmy Dean

_____

_____

_____

_____

_____

_____

_____

_____

_____

_____

_____

_____

6

Henry Was a Mess

We human beings are indeed an interesting lot. We all like to think we're unique, different, carry a bigger burden than most, and are more committed than the other guy or gal. While all of us are different, we're also in many ways the same. Regardless of where my business opportunities have taken me in the past twenty years, I've found these observations are true.

All of us know that everyone carries what they perceive to be a rather full load in life. There is one particular group, however, which I have a special affinity for. These are the good people who try so very hard in life but never seem to get it together!

Not long ago, a manager told me about a gentleman who was nearing retirement. He said, "Joe, Henry has been with me for almost twenty years now, and I swear I've never seen anyone try so hard and mess up so much!" The manager went on to explain how Henry was never absent, had a great attitude, but for all his efforts, never seemed to ever master anything.

After hearing about Henry, I asked the obvious question, "Why have you kept him on for twenty years if he's caused you so many problems?"

The manager thought a minute, laughed, and said, "I guess because as strange as it may sound to you, Joe, Henry's really a leader with all my people. They all respect and like him because he tries so hard."

What an interesting observation on that manager's part. Henry's attitude and work ethic were worth everyone of his mess-ups and mistakes. He even said he hated to lose him to retirement.

I had the opportunity of meeting Henry just before he retired. From that brief encounter, I know that I couldn't have fired Henry either. He just smiled his sincere smile and said, "Mr. Black, this is the best place in the world to work. I wish I could stay twenty more years." His boss, standing next to Henry, hugged him and said, "Yeah, Henry, I really wish you could stay, too." He meant it—Henry was a mess, but he was also a leader.

JUST NOTES

_____
_____
_____
_____
_____
_____

"Just as there are no little people or unimportant lives, there is no insignificant work."

Elena Bonner

_____
_____
_____
_____
_____
_____
_____
_____
_____
_____
_____
_____

25

7

Are You a True Leader?

The other day while I was watching one of the major network newscasts, the commentator began talking about the "leader" of a small, Third World country. As the newsman read his script, it became obvious to me that this leader wasn't a leader at all. I've always liked my own simple definition: "A leader is anyone who chooses to set a positive example for others to follow." I like this because it's the truth. And according to this definition, anyone can be a leader.

Think about someone you admire, love, and respect. Using this definition, isn't this person a leader? Webster's Dictionary has half a page on the words lead and leader, but it doesn't have our definition. One can be a president of a country, a member of congress, a senator, a chair of the board, etc., and still not be a leader. You and I can each decide to be true leaders if we choose each day to set a positive example for others to follow. Very likely, some of the best mentors you know have never made a lot of money. They've never held a high post in government or business, been on TV or radio, and have never thought of themselves as leaders.

Real leaders are often like that. They simply go about the daily tasks of life dealing with realities in a constructive fashion and setting positive examples for others to follow. The next time you see on television or read about dictators, enforcers, managers, prime ministers, premiers, presidents, or kings, ask yourself: "Are they really leaders?" Then, smile and say to yourself, "I've chosen to be a real leader. I hope they have too."

One other thing—if you choose to be a leader, you've chosen to be a hero, too. The choice is yours. Why not be a hero starting today?

JUST NOTES

"A good leader can't get too far ahead of his followers."

Franklin D. Roosevelt

8

Walking Our Own High Wires

To me, the circus smelled like it did in the 1950s. The big tent, clean sawdust, well-kept animals–it was like stepping back in time. I was in Vienna, Austria, when I learned that a circus was in the nearby countryside. I simply had to go. The tent was huge with three rings and all the trappings of the old Ringling Brothers' circus of days gone by. Memories flooded my mind of the days before Ringling performed in air-conditioned arenas. The circus came to town, and an open field was transformed overnight into a Disneyland, and then disappeared as fast as it had appeared.

In Vienna, the high-wire artist stole the show. A silence fell over the audience as the drum rolled and the artist began his walk high above the center of the rings. I could hardly watch. You see, there was no net, no guy wire attached to the man, and no people standing under him to break his fall if the unthinkable should happen.

Slowly and deliberately, he made his perfect walk. The audience exploded with applause as he climbed down the rope ladder to our comfort zone. It amazed me and still does to see these athletes tease death.

After the performance I asked a circus employee, whom I heard speaking English, "How long has that high wire artist been performing in your circus?" The answer was, "Five years." I followed with another question, "How long has it been since you lost a performer?" He replied, "Five years."

I began to think about that. In the United States, the high-wire artists I've seen have a safety net or a guy wire to save them if they fall. Let me now ask you a question. If you were employed by a circus in Austria and a circus in the United States, for which one would you try harder to do it right the first time? "That's easy," you'd say. "For obvious reasons, I'd try harder for the circus which provides no safety nets or guy wires."

In the United States, because we're pretty darn good at building nets to catch our errors on our jobs, we tend to fall off a lot. Perhaps it's time we do it right the first time and stop relying on our safety wires. If I'm going to buy a ticket to the circus, I'll buy the Vienna ticket any day–that's true quality and dedication.

Does that same logic apply to cars and other products made overseas? If we Americans want to be the best, we must take away that net and care enough to do our jobs right every time. We all walk the high wire. Let's not fall off. We simply no longer have that luxury in the world marketplace!

"The toughest thing about success is that you've got to keep on being a success."

Irving Berlin

9

―――――――――――――――――――――――――――

Spring People

The rippling brook flowing by our mountain home carries cool, clear spring water. I've followed it to its source. A beautiful spring bubbles out of the earth high atop the mountain. I first visited this place in 1951 when I hiked along the top of the mountain with my father, aunt, and uncle.

Today, the water flows just as fully and clearly as it did when I was a boy. For almost forty years this lovely spring has provided our mountain home with a plentiful source of water. It runs through a water line directly from the spring down a steep ravine to holding tanks.

Most of our neighbors in that mountain valley have drilled expensive wells and installed electrical pumps to meet their water needs. These wells require a switch to start the pump, and only then will the water flow into their homes. However, at our house no switch is needed; we simply turn on the tap and there it is!

Many people I know are a lot like the well. They require an outside force to turn them on before they're able to give their best in their professional and personal lives. Then there are those who don't need an external power source to turn them on.

I call them "spring people" because they give of their best every day, day after day, just like our spring atop the mountain. I've discovered that spring people are the happiest, most positive, most productive, and most giving people; they often help turn on the switches of the "well people."

Each of us has a choice: we can either be a spring person or a well person. Think about it—which are you?

JUST NOTES

_____

_____

_____

_____

_____

_____

"Success isn't a result of spontaneous combustion. You must set yourself on fire."

Arnold Glasow

_____

_____

_____

_____

_____

_____

_____

_____

_____

_____

_____

_____

10

Aren't Mistakes Great?

All people, even those who achieve some measure of success in their lives, have made mistakes. Mistakes allow us to learn lessons our successes rarely teach us. I often ask groups in seminars this question: "How many of you have learned more from your mistakes than from your successes?" A vast majority of hands go up every time.

Everyone makes mistakes. The key is to learn from them and move forward, hopefully a wiser person. I've heard the best way not to make mistakes is to do nothing. This is true. Doing nothing, however, is the greatest mistake of all. To do nothing at all is a nuclear mistake, not a conventional one.

Have you known students who suffered a nervous disorder if they didn't make straight A's in school? Have you known golfers who cursed unless every shot was perfect? The list goes on and on. Learning to cope with the fact that we human beings are not perfect is perhaps one of the most important lessons in life. We'd all do well to learn early in life to accept defeat, learn from it, and move on in a positive way. Striving to do or to be our best is certainly a goal to aspire to, both in our personal and professional lives. But striving to be absolutely perfect may send us to the nut house, the outhouse, or maybe an early grave.

Those who have attempted really to live life—not just exist—have made many mistakes and probably have a few bones, if not entire skeletons, in their closets. I know I've made my share of big and small mistakes, personally and professionally. I'm sure my dogs would enjoy a visit to my closet, as there are many bones there! So what? To live life means to make mistakes as well as enjoy success. If we do, we'll accept both our mistakes and successes and become better people.

So, see how many mistakes you make today. If you make several, you're probably accomplishing a lot and achieving success. Mistakes—may you continue to make them. Just be sure they're not the same ones you made before!

JUST NOTES

_____

_____

_____

_____

_____

_____

"Notice the difference between what happens when a man says to himself, 'I have failed three times,' and what happens when he says, 'I am a failure.'"

S. I. Hayakawa

_____

_____

_____

_____

_____

_____

_____

_____

_____

_____

_____

_____

11

Thinking the Worst

The seminar was almost ready to begin when he walked in, marched down the center aisle, and took a seat on the second row just to the right of center. I stood there adjusting my lavaliere mike and scanning the 100-plus people in the group. Most of them I had met and spoken with as they entered. The "salt of the earth" people had come to this quality seminar with excitement, fear, curiosity, and many other emotions.

This particular individual, who had arrived late and sat in the second row, obviously didn't want to be there. His shaved head and earring stood out as he sat down and quickly and deliberately threw both feet onto the empty Samsonite chair in front of him. Then he stared at me as if to say, "Okay, sucker, change my mind!"

When the seminar began, his cold stare didn't melt. As always, the group included a variety of individuals–some who would believe anything I said, some who were very skeptical, and others who truly wanted to learn something.

Glancing over the crowd during the first hour of lecture before the break, I noticed the hostile one continued his icy stare. I felt antagonism toward this young rebel, who obviously would like nothing better than to tell me exactly what I could do with my quality process.

Never changing his expression or taking his eyes off me, he refused to participate in any of the warm-up events, such as shaking hands with those around him or sharing his full name and where he was born. "Why are some people so negative?" I found myself thinking. "Why do so many young people act as if they simply do not give a good damn about anything?" Finally, the first hour of our four-hour seminar was completed.

At break, while I arranged the video, slide projector, and handout materials for the next hour, I saw the young man coming towards me. At that time, I decided to invite him to leave if he didn't wish to be a part of his team.

"Can I talk with you, sir?" he said.

I answered, "Certainly."

Then, this arrogant young rebel, with tears in his eyes, said, "Mr. Black, I was up all last night with my nine-year-old girl. She has sickle cell anemia and isn't doing well at all. I'm so tired and I'm trying hard to stay awake. I just wanted you to know. Oh, I'm enjoying your talk, too." Then he turned and walked away.

Joe Black, the expert! The positive leader who has the opportunity to influence thousands of individuals had blown it! When will I stop making assumptions and putting people into neat little boxes? When will I stop being prejudiced toward people who are different from me? Over the past twenty or so years, I've made progress in accepting other people as they are. But I still have miles to go in learning to love more and judge less the hard-to-love humans on this planet. My perceptions are often so wrong. If I had been in this young man's shoes, I probably wouldn't have even attended the seminar. The real "heroes" of the world really do often go unnoticed and unappreciated.

JUST NOTES

"Be kind. Remember everyone you meet is fighting a hard battle."

T. H. Thompson

12

A 'Coon-Hunting Mule

Not long ago I spent several days at a beautiful place called Mid Pines Resort in Southern Pines, North Carolina. Because the area is famous for its exceptional golf courses, many people choose to retire there. I was there to do a team-building session with a large company. For two full days we worked and ate together, but didn't make time for golf, which I regret.

One gentleman in our group, upon discovering that occasionally I like to fish and hunt, began to tell me a racoon-hunting story. He told me he had a friend who had a mule trained to hunt 'coons! He said the mule would actually climb under or jump over a fence to get to a 'coon he was after. This man was serious. He even offered to take me out and introduce me to the mule and its owner. Unfortunately, time didn't allow me to meet that mule, but I hope to someday.

It seems the local gentry, with their fine well-bred horses, were amazed at this mule, and some had even offered to buy it. One fellow said he wanted to take the mule on the David Letterman television show. This mule probably will never rise to national stardom, and I really hope he doesn't. I'd like to keep some Americana down home on the farm away from the television shows and the media.

Somewhere, though, there's a mule I respect for his commitment to meet his goal. He'll go over, under, or through any obstacle to get what he's after. Call it stubborn, but we could all use a little focused stubbornness to help us catch the 'coons in our lives. I'll certainly remember that Carolina mule the next time I'm trying hard to reach a goal.

JUST NOTES

"One may walk over the highest mountain—one step at a time."

John Wanamaker

13

The Kid Was Too Smart

My wife and I often travel together, frequently on airplanes. Although today's aviation is a modern miracle technically, it's often horse and buggy in the way passengers are treated by the airlines. But that's another subject entirely.

One Sunday evening, my wife and I boarded a plane at LaGuardia in New York City, headed for Charlotte, North Carolina. Soon after we were seated in 6A and 6B, a family of three came in and sat directly behind us. They were a handsome family consisting of mother, father, and young son—about seven. Mother asked Father if he had surgery scheduled for Monday morning, to which he replied a polite, "Yes."

Then it was time for "Let's share with all the people around us how smart Tommy is." Mother began to talk to Tommy about hypothermia and how it's treated—my goodness, she's a doctor, too! Perhaps Tommy is not their child, but a midget brain surgeon. Tommy then began using such big words I felt like taking him to the plane lavatory and washing his mouth out with soap!

He was a brilliant child who knew the adult world very well. He asked questions of his mother that only doctors and medical students might know to ask. If the plane had crashed and I were injured, I wouldn't have screamed, "Doctor!" I would have called for Tommy.

By then, everyone around us who was still awake knew Tommy was no ordinary kid. The mother and Tommy had carried on a conversation about a variety of subjects which left no doubt that he would grow up to be the next Louis Pasteur.

When we landed in Charlotte and while his mother beamed, he compared the approach and landing to hundreds of others he had experienced. After we pulled up to the gate, father, mother, and Tommy deplaned for further adventures in life.

During the entire trip, there had been no mention of Christmas—just a week past—other children, school, toys, friends, or Dad. Tommy had only talked about himself and all the things he knew. Boy, was I glad when we landed. Kids—I love them and want them to study and make all A's and B's, but I want them to be children for a few years. Perhaps one of the greatest gifts a parent can give children is to let them be children, at least from LaGuardia to Charlotte.

Tommy, wherever you are, I wish you luck and happiness. I also hope you will learn to love others and give to those around you. Not just your mind, but also your heart.

JUST NOTES

_____

_____

_____

_____

_____

_____

"A great man is he who has not lost the heart of a child."

Mencries

_____

_____

_____

_____

_____

_____

_____

_____

_____

_____

_____

_____

_____

14

What a Shot

I took a five-iron out of my golf bag with all the confidence of Arnold Palmer in his younger days. While my wife and her sister stood watching, I addressed the ball on the last hole on the nine-hole golf course in Tryon, North Carolina. I also noticed five or six "old timers," including the golf pro, watching from the club house.

I swung and it felt great. The ball climbed into the sky towards the number nine, par three hole. It flew past the creek, missed the limbs on the trees, and dropped right by the flag, rolling about six inches from the hole! I held my pose at the tee almost as if I wanted the swing to last forever. My wife and her sister exclaimed about how wonderful a shot it was, and I thanked them. I knew the onlookers were also talking about my fantastic shot. Oh, I was proud!

My wife hit her shot into the creek, and her sister did the same. After I helped both of them retrieve their balls, they chipped up onto the green. Then I marked my ball and let them putt out with two double bogeys. Placing my ball on my mark, I stepped back to study my putt–a straight shot in for a birdie. The old timers were still watching as I confidently approached the ball with my putter. After taking a practice stroke, I prepared for *the* putt for a beautiful birdie—one under par! I stroked the ball gently and ran it past the hole a good ten inches or more! I couldn't believe my miss, but I calmly walked around and putted the ball into the hole for a par.

As I walked off the green to the clubhouse, an old gentleman who had been watching said, "Black, that was a great tee shot—sorry you blew the birdie." I thanked him, then went in the clubhouse to cool off and drink a coke with my wife and her sister.

When you stop to think about it, sometimes life can be like that golf shot. Sure, I should have made the putt for a birdie, but I didn't. I still parred the hole, which for me is very good. Why couldn't the gentleman have said, "Nice par, Black." Well, you and I both know why. He knew how much I wanted that birdie, and he wanted me to know he cared. Sometimes, though, when I've failed to measure up to my potential, it would be refreshing to hear someone say, "Nice par, Black; you'll make that birdie next time."

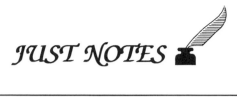

JUST NOTES

_____

_____

_____

_____

_____

_____

_____

"You can't build a reputation on what you are going to do."

Henry Ford

_____

_____

_____

_____

_____

_____

_____

_____

_____

_____

_____

_____

_____

15

Sunday Nights

Sunday night...do you look forward to Sunday night? I don't know if I've ever heard anyone say, "I can hardly wait until Sunday night." People seem to feel that the last vestiges of the freedom they enjoy on the weekend will finally shrivel up and die Sunday night. Then it's back to the grind on Monday. The squirters of the world will be out hunting for you then, hiding and waiting to hose you down with deadlines, problems, and negative trash.

What a bleak way to go through life. Consider the alternative prospects: no one needs you on Monday, nobody cares where you are, no opportunities wait for you, there are no new people to meet and interact with. Now, that would be depressing. To be able to get up, to be healthy enough to go do our thing, is good reason to be excited on Sunday night!

One suggestion: Sunday night, spend twenty minutes or so counting your blessings. Take some time alone away from the television and radio to think–think positively. The people you meet on Monday will be glad you did. You may even help them begin to look forward to another new beginning–every Monday. Happy Monday, and may you have many more.

JUST NOTES

"Problems are only opportunities in work clothes."

Henry J. Kaiser

16

Corporate Prenatal Care

Today we hear a lot about the importance of prenatal care for expectant mothers. They're urged not to drink alcohol, smoke, or use any drugs. We know now that a mother's diet, environment, and exercise habits can have a significant impact on the future health and well-being of her child.

What could these facts possibly have to do with companies attempting to implement quality processes? A great deal. You see, the company is the mother and the quality process is the fetus. Company managers can kill the delicate structure of change and growth. Nurturing must take place if the unborn child is really to be born and grow up to be a strong and healthy adult.

Leaders in companies understand this. Many managers who are not true leaders don't. Just as the mother may choose to abuse her body while carrying the child, the manager may dump negative trash on the quality process by his or her words or deeds. It's up to leaders in companies to understand that after nine months or so, their quality processes are really just being born. They must feed and nurture the young quality process by appropriate behavior in how they manage and continue to rear the quality child for the rest of its life.

If we're not too busy to observe and listen, the world of mothers and babies can teach us a lot in the business world. If you have a sickly quality process in your place of business, perhaps you should take a good look at the mother's habits.

JUST NOTES

"The child is father of the man."

Wordsworth

17

No Victims Here

Recently, during a team-building session with a group of top managers in New York City, I heard an extremely interesting comment. This was an intensive two-day workshop on how to make good teams better.

After the morning session of the first day, one excited analytical type came up to me and said, "Joe, we've had a lot of battles on our team over the years, but no victims." Now, that's a profound statement!

At the end of the two-day session, it was very clear why this gentleman's statement was correct. Each member of his team accepted the others as they were, listened respectfully to all perspectives, trusted the others, and had a high care and love ratio for the group. They fine-tuned their attitudes and skills and identified new ways to better serve each other and their external customers.

We're going to do the team session with them again next year. They are not only the best, they want to get even better. "*No Victims*"–I like that, and come to think of it, that's the way it is on most great teams.

JUST NOTES

_____

_____

_____

_____

_____

_____

"A company is known by the people it employs."

Unknown

_____

_____

_____

_____

_____

_____

_____

_____

_____

_____

_____

_____

18

Two Fat Lovers

There they were. Two large—no, two fat people—sat in a booth enjoying seafood plates together. I noticed them as the waitress seated me in the next booth facing them. As I looked over the menu, I couldn't help hearing the two talking.

"Wouldn't it be romantic," she said, "to meet you at the Beacon Drive-In for some onion rings when I get off?"

"Sure," he replied. "If that makes you happy, then I'll be there."

These folks weren't mushy or falling all over each other or holding hands. They were plain people in their mid-forties. As their conversation continued, they talked of ordinary things as we all do every day, but they spoke of them as if they were big events in their lives. Such excitement about the routine began to interest and amaze me. Grocery shopping was discussed with such enthusiasm that I started to ask if I could join them. Family, the Christmas tree, presents—all were discussed as if they were kids again. By then, I had ordered my meal, eaten it, had a cup of coffee and asked for my check.

As I prepared to leave, my two new fat friends were leaving also. While we stood in line together at the cash register, she adjusted his old blue jean jacket, told him he looked nice, and reminded him not to forget the cake mix for mama. Their stomachs met as he pecked her on the nose with a gentle, loving kiss.

I noticed that he carried a radio and a little lunch box. Perhaps he was going to eat again in the car! I don't know where he was headed next, maybe to work, but I do know they were to meet for dinner at the drive-in. I also know they were married. As I paid my check, I watched as they walked out the door holding hands and then parted to go their separate ways.

Two people, living out their lives like you and me, perhaps with one exception. It seemed to me they were real people, not concerned with current fads or with what people thought about them. They were just happy and very much in love. They enjoyed the little things in life most of us take for granted. I don't mind telling you–I am envious of them.

JUST NOTES

"God must love the common man; he made so many of them."

Abraham Lincoln

19

The Lady in Red

It was a beautiful fall day in Arkansas, not far from Little Rock. We were into the second day of a quality seminar with a Fortune 500 company, and things were really working! At break time, a very attractive middle-aged woman called out to me, "Joe Black, come over here!" She had participated well in the sessions, but it was apparent she was now upset about something.

I said, "Yes, ma'am, what can I do for you?"

"Joe, I agree with everything we've said and done over the last two days," she said. "But I just can't hold it in any more. Do you see that lady in the red blouse over by the Coke machine? She doesn't do pee-diddly-squat around here and she makes the same money I do! I don't know who she has an eight-by-ten glossy of, but if she's not fired, I'm going to quit and go work somewhere else!"

She went on and on about what a lazy, no-good person this particular female manager was. Finally, after she had wound down, I asked her if I could speak.

Calmly and deliberately I looked this woman in the eye and said, "If what you say is true, I can understand why you feel as you do about that lady. But have you stopped to think that if you leave your company and go to work somewhere else because of that lady in red, you will meet one of her brothers or sisters, because they are everywhere! You see, every company has its ladies or men in red. The key is learning how to deal effectively with them on a daily basis."

After a moment she smiled at me and said, "I guess you're right, Joe. I've never really thought about it that way, but it still makes me mad."

All of us have our lady in red no matter where we work or what we do. The trick is being able to manage our own behavior to deal with these types of people. One thing is certain—we can't change them. The only thing you and I can do is set a positive example for others and understand that we must be wise enough to deal with difficult people. Don't let a lady in red ruin your career!

JUST NOTES

"The most difficult thing in the world is to know how to do a thing and to watch someone else doing it wrong, without comment."

Theodore H. White

20

Points for the Team

It was hot at the Clemson football stadium that September day. Over 80,000 fanatical fans had gathered at "Death Valley" (appropriately named) to enjoy another in a long string of Clemson Tiger victories on the gridiron. With the temperature in the 90s, I had a bad sunburn by the end of the third quarter and had to get some relief from the heat and the crowd. I told my wife, Kathy, I needed a large Coca-cola with a lot of ice or I would die. She begged me to bring her one, too.

Now, get the picture–Clemson doesn't have the football, it's the fourth quarter, and Clemson is behind seven points! It was a perfect time to leave.

I walked through a stadium exit into the shade under the arena and ordered two large Cokes filled with ice. About that time, I heard a tremendous roar from the crowd. How could Clemson have scored? They didn't even have the ball a few seconds ago! I soon learned that a Clemson player had intercepted a pass and run it in for a touchdown. I hurried to a stadium entrance and stood there hunched over so those around me could still see the game. Clemson was going for a two-point conversion which would put them one point ahead.

Now, I'm a happily married man, but as I stood there with a Coke in each hand, I couldn't help noticing one of the most beautiful female human beings I had ever laid eyes on, standing about one foot to my right. She was *gorgeous*. She had on a sun dress, and let me say, I think she was tan all over!

At that moment, Clemson lined up, ran one of their big backs up the middle, and made the two points. The next thing I knew, that gorgeous girl turned to me, put one tan hand on one side of my red head, the other tan hand on the other side of my red head, and kissed me on the mouth like I ain't never been kissed! I mean—she laid one on me. I stood there in a daze and thought, "Oh, God, I wish they'd score again!"

She then ran down the steps and I went back to my seat. Kathy said, "Joe, where have you been?" I replied, "Kathy, drink your Coke; you wouldn't believe me if I told you!" Clemson went on to win and you're probably wondering if I ever saw that girl again. No, I haven't, but I'm still looking for her!

This really happened and I did enjoy it. It's also an interesting commentary on our lives. On impulse, a perfect stranger turns to another perfect stranger, kisses him very hard and runs off because some team scored an extra point. After pondering this, I started thinking about work.

Working people just like you and me score touchdowns, make extra points, and kick long field goals every day on the job, and what do we usually get? Usually a, "That's what we pay them for." That's it! Well, that's pathetic. Isn't it funny that we get so excited at sports events, but don't stop to cheer our teams at home or at work where the points do count?

Recognition is something everyone needs. It's the best fuel I know to keep people going. I'm not suggesting you kiss people or jump up and down and applaud when they do well. I'm simply suggesting that the real heroes, the people who win every day, need recognition as much or more than any athletic team does.

The teams of which you are a part need to be cheered, too. Don't wait for someone else—start yourself by finding someone doing something right and thanking that person for it. A sincere "Thank you; I appreciate this specific point you scored for the team," will mean more than a kiss-and-run incident. It may even feel as good, though that might be stretching it a little.

Thanks—I appreciate you. There. That felt good!

JUST NOTES

_____

_____

_____

_____

_____

_____

"We can't all be heroes because someone has to sit on the curb and clap as they go by."

Will Rogers

_____

_____

_____

_____

_____

_____

_____

_____

_____

_____

_____

_____

21

We Need Those Second and Third Stringers Too

I recently heard a presentation by a business consultant in which he compared business with the world of sports. Several interesting contrasts were drawn that are worth noting.

In sports, you always know the score, but in business you often don't know who's winning. Recognition and praise are immediate in sporting events, but in the work world, recognition is often infrequent and inadequate. Also, in the work world, you don't always know the rules of the game, and when you think you do, they change! To the contrary, the sports world has rules that are constant and clearly understood by all participants.

After this session, I thought of another key issue the consultant could have addressed. On most athletic teams the coaches have the opportunity to play only the first string. The best of the bench, barring injuries, are usually on the field until a comfortable lead is gained against the opponents. On the other hand, in the business world the coaches must play their first, second, and third strings together everyday to beat the competition.

Some people play their best and still remain on the second or third teams. But I realized that day, second and third stringers, if performing to their maximum potential, are truly first stringers in their own unique way. We must remember our second and third stringers get much of the work done while the first stringers lead the way.

Being a good follower and doing one's best can be just as important as being on the first team. Recognition of the second and third teams, as well as the first team, is critical if the entire squad is to be a cohesive unit and accomplish a given task. Good coaches in business and athletics know that simple fact. It's worth remembering.

JUST NOTES

"The rising tide lifts all the boats."

John F. Kennedy

22

Ride 'Em, Cowboy

The streams of light through the Carolina pines made a beautiful setting for a trail ride. Deciding to go for a Labor Day trek not far from our home, my wife and I saddled up our horses, Rusty and Star, and headed out for a five-mile ride. Since it was an unusually warm day, the horses seemed as pleased as we were to steal away into the cool calmness of the woods.

Soon we were moving deeper and deeper into the pine forest on a narrow-cut trail. The only sounds were the horses' footsteps and an occasional horse word or two between Rusty and Star. Rusty and I were following behind when I noticed Star dancing a jig in front of us. It reminded me of a performing rodeo or circus horse doing a cha-cha. Then Rusty began the dance as well. I then realized that this was no performance but a reaction to yellow-jackets! Star had stepped into their hole and stirred them to an angry frenzy.

Those yellow-jackets were now coming out of the hole by the hundreds and swarming all over poor Rusty's head and body! He began to thrash wildly against a pine tree in an attempt to get away from them. One of my legs was slammed against the pine tree as well. It all happened so quickly, I hardly had time to think.

Still trying to escape, Rusty bolted down the narrow path, while I looked for a way to avoid the fast-approaching tree limbs. Rusty was in a full run when I left the saddle and dived off into a small clearing. I hit the ground hard and lay there a moment collecting my wits. There were no yellow-jackets on me, but my glasses were gone.

Fearing possible broken or fractured bones, I moved very slowly and managed to sit up. I then heard my wife Kathy yelling to ask if I was hurt. I was alright but a bit shaken. She agreed to ride on through the woods and into a nearby peach orchard to search for Rusty while I searched for my glasses. To my amazement, I found them intact, put them on, and walked out into the peach orchard.

After five or ten minutes of looking for my wife and my horse, I whistled loudly and heard a reply in the distance. Kathy had found Rusty rolling in the grass between the peach trees. Fortunately, he was unhurt except for a few stings, but his saddle was hanging upside down around his belly with one stirrup missing. After rolling, Rusty had galloped away toward the highway. Pulling a Dale Evans feat, Kathy had raced alongside him, reached for his reins and pulled him to a stop.

When I finally caught up with them, I experienced both relief and excitement. I was relieved to find we were all okay, and excited that through sheer luck, we had come through what could have been a very bad situation.

I know many people who are comfortable in their saddles, riding along the beautiful trails they have fought so hard to ride. Sooner or later for most, the yellow-jackets rush out. They come in many forms, such as broken careers, unfair bosses, illness, loss of loved ones, depression, boredom, drugs, divorce, problems with their children–the list goes on and on. My point is: sometimes it takes more courage to jump off than to stay on.

Many of us have experienced situations where we know we should jump off into a clearing in the woods. To stay on board may mean life-crippling falls or even death. Don't misunderstand me; I admire folks who stay in the saddle and "ride 'em, cowboy, ride 'em" if the cost isn't too great. We must all work through the crises in our lives. However, when yellow-jackets cover our heads and company presidents, bosses, or family and friends forget their precious rider is depending on them, it may be time to leave. It could be time to jump off and walk out into the orchard.

JUST NOTES

_____

_____

_____

_____

_____

_____

"If you want to succeed, you should strike out on new paths rather than travel the worn paths of accepted success."

John D. Rockefeller

_____

_____

_____

_____

_____

_____

_____

_____

_____

_____

_____

23

Big Slack Attack

Late one Sunday night, two of my business associates and I began the long drive from the airport in Memphis, Tennessee, to central Mississippi. We were headed south just out of Memphis when we realized none of us had eaten since lunch. Looming on the horizon were the famous golden arches, but as I'm not a fan of fast food, I asked my friends if there was a real restaurant en route to Mississippi. Familiar with the drive, they assured me this would be our last chance to eat anything for at least two hours. So we turned in to the parking lot at McDonald's, got out of our car, and walked inside.

Standing behind the counter were five uniformed employees–too busy talking with each other to acknowledge our presence. With large rear ends and stomachs to match, they all looked as if they had been eating fast food since birth. After a minute or two my friends and I were simply amazed that not one of these employees asked to take our orders. In the throes of a "Big Slack Attack," they behaved as if we didn't exist. As we looked up at the lighted menu over their heads, they continued to ignore us.

After another minute or two, I had a brainstorm. Since those five employees seemed to lack common courtesy or any desire for our business, I thought I would have some fun with them.

Interrupting their conversation, I boldly announced, "I want you all to know we are McDonald's inspectors, and we don't appreciate being treated in this manner!" All five jumped to attention. They began cooking fries that had not been ordered, slinging hamburgers left and right, and scrubbing clean grills. One of them even asked if he could take our order.

We got our food, ate it, and left–never to return. As we drove away into the Mississippi night, one of my friends began laughing. "Joe," he said, "I can't believe you told those people we were McDonald's inspectors!"

I replied, "My friend, we *are* McDonald's inspectors. *We are the customers.*"

When you are in a place of business, whether it be a restaurant, a gas station, a clothing store or a supermarket, remember you are also an inspector. In fact, you are the only inspector that counts, for *you are the customer.* Looking at your own organization, who's inspecting your workplace?

JUST NOTES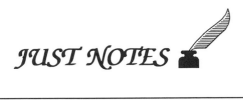

_____

_____

_____

_____

_____

_____

"People can be divided into three groups: those who make things happen, those who watch things happen, and those who wonder what happened."

John M. Newbern

_____

_____

_____

_____

_____

_____

_____

_____

_____

_____

_____

24

Her Eyes Were Like Steel

It was a cold morning in New York City when I stepped out of my hotel on Park Avenue. At 8:30, I was going out to call on two customers, both located a block or two over on 6th Avenue (the Avenue of the Americas). As I crossed 5th Avenue and walked past the New York Public Library, I turned down the street to the Avenue of the Americas. I noticed several street people were still scattered along the sidewalk where they'd spent the night. By now, most had moved over to the fence behind the library so as not to be in the direct path of the thundering herds walking past them.

Although I had made that trip and taken that walk many times, I'd never before really noticed the street people. Perhaps there was a larger group that morning. These people were of all ages—young, middle-aged, and older.

As I walked along on this particular morning, I couldn't help noticing them because several were in my path. Most were covered to their heads, trying to stay warm. One bag lady looked at me with steely eyes. Instead of simply stepping around her as I drew towards her, I looked at her. Her skin was like leather, and her clothes were mostly rags. A quilt covered her from neck to waist and three bags surrounded her lower body.

Reaching her, for no reason I know, I stopped (a thing you do not do in New York City), and a "Hello" fell from my mouth. She said nothing, so I resumed walking, thinking she must be on drugs or something.

Then I felt someone pull on my overcoat, and turning quickly, faced a well-dressed businessman, who said, "I believe that lady there wants to see you about something." I looked and saw her still staring at me. Against my better judgment, I returned ten or fifteen steps to see what she wanted.

She burned her steel-gray eyes into mine and with a smile held out her cold hand and said, "Thank you for speaking to me, Mister." She released my hand, pulled her blanket over her head, and curled up in the fetal position. I turned and walked on to the Avenue of the Americas.

I did visit my customers and had a successful trip. But I don't remember what our business meetings were about. What I do remember is that I walk past the needy of the world every day and don't have a satisfactory answer as to why I ignore them. A kind word obviously meant a great deal to one poor soul.

A great teacher once said: "Whatever you do unto the least of these, my brothers, you do also unto me." I often think about that, but thinking about it doesn't change a thing unless I turn my thoughts into positive actions. Think about it, then do something about it...that's the key.

JUST NOTES

_____

_____

_____

_____

_____

_____

"Many eyes go through the meadow, but few see the flowers in it."

Ralph Waldo Emerson

_____

_____

_____

_____

_____

_____

_____

_____

_____

_____

_____

_____

25

Fortunes to be Made by Caring

I dislike shopping malls. I believe there's a book called *The Malling of America*. I haven't read it, but I think I know what it's about. The downtowns of many towns, small and large, are dying out. Gone forever are the special smells of the old store on Main Street, and gone, too, are most of the special people who ran them–the community of merchants.

From my childhood, I remember Wink Parrott's Food Palace, Bivens' Hardware, Alexander's Feed and Seed, and Leo Few's Barber Shop. I also remember the Post Office (when it truly served the public), Wylie's Department Store, and the Rexall Drug Store, with the same druggist always on duty.

You and I both know America will never go back to that simple time. That's reality. But I really miss the attitude of the people who managed those stores and businesses.

A. They were glad you were there and appreciated your business
B. They truly cared about you as a person

C. They had the customer's best interest in mind
D. They had integrity

There are still good folks in the retail and service businesses. Some progressive towns are trying to preserve the special environment and service of a bygone era. Big chains like Wal-Mart do it right; they seem to care when I shop there. Sears and K mart, on the other hand, don't appear to care much about me as a customer. Delta Airlines seems to care, but in my opinion, US Air doesn't.

It's an attitude. What I want is for people who run businesses to care about me as a person. I'll pay more for that service. There are fortunes to be made simply by caring and by being courteous.

JUST NOTES

"*Life is not so short but that there is always time for courtesy.*"

Ralph Waldo Emerson

26

The Magic of Trees

Last weekend, my wife and I planted a tree I dug up from the deep woods close to our home. I don't know who owns the land—mostly a big gully—so I dug up the beautiful fifteen foot beech.

After manhandling it onto my trusty 1958 Ford truck, we brought it home. Kathy sat in the bed of the truck, carefully holding the tree in a wash tub. We got "tons" of dirt with the roots. You know how that goes. After digging a hole big enough to bury an NFL linebacker, I carefully placed the soil, roots, and tree in. We then put the dirt back over it, tapped it down, and watered the tree.

Oh yes, I also named that tree; we give names to all the trees we plant. This particular tree is special. Its name is Wellons in honor of a wonderful young friend who responded positively to being uprooted in her life.

Planting a tree is good for you. First, you get some exercise (and how!). Second, you feel great when you step back and look at it. Third, you get to water it, fertilize it, and watch it grow.

I've planted many trees in my 44 years of life. Sure, a few haven't made it, but most have. What is it about planting a tree that's so special? I guess it's knowing that it probably will be there to be enjoyed long after I'm gone. Trees are necessary for our very survival as humans. They remind us we're all in this together.

By the way, I talk to my trees, too. Some talk back as they grow and I love it. Recently, one asked me to hang a swing among her branches someday. I promised I would. And I swear that tree is growing faster now, obviously looking forward to some occasional company in that swing.

Now, get a little crazy and plant a tree; watch it grow, and enjoy. I'll lay ten to one odds you'll be glad you did. I wish for you many shady summer days!

JUST NOTES

_____

_____

_____

_____

_____

_____

"Who plants trees loves others besides himself."

Unknown

_____

_____

_____

_____

_____

_____

_____

_____

_____

_____

_____

_____

27

A Yellowstone Night

Ice formed on my eyelashes as the winter winds of Yellowstone National Park blew across the high plateau of Wyoming. My wife and I had snowmobiled some 50 miles to the Old Faithful Inn from the park headquarters at Mammoth Hot Springs. We got there just in time to see Old Faithful shoot hot water high into the snowy winter sky. By then, our fingertips were frigid even in our heavy ski gloves.

After some discussion, we agreed to ride a snow coach, a tracked tank-like vehicle, back to Mammoth Hot Springs. The snow coach was heated, but was very slow, we were told. The driver and five passengers sat in the engine front car, and our car was connected and followed. We had the services of a radio to communicate with the front.

Finding our seats, we settled in with eight other tourists from Oregon. They were a tightly knit group who had been dropped off on the way to Old Faithful to cross-country ski the rest of the way in. As we rode, we listened to stories of cross-country skiing experiences as the Nordic Club members shared stories with one another. My wife Kathy and I tried to have some conversation with this group, but they seemed to prefer their own company.

As darkness fell, we bumped along with the headlights of the snow coach as our only light. After awhile, we heard the sound of a harmonica. One of the party in the front car was playing it and broadcasting over the radio to our car. Rolling along in the snow to "My Old Kentucky Home" and "Oh, Susannah" was peaceful and welcomed by all.

When someone suggested that we sing some old songs, the two cars tuned in to each other via radio and we began singing, "You Are My Sunshine." Almost immediately, the barriers between us began to melt. Within five minutes, it was no longer the Nordic Ski Club and Kathy and Joe, but the "Singing Coach of Yellowstone." For almost two hours we sang and laughed and talked with one another in the dark December night.

Finally we arrived, singing and hungry, back at our hotel in Mammoth Hot Springs. As the lights came on and we departed, everyone in both cars made an effort to introduce themselves to the others. Kathy and I saw their faces, and they saw ours. We had bonded on that long ride. The next morning many of the club members came by our table as we enjoyed breakfast. We spoke several more times before we left the park the next day.

Isn't it interesting how singing together helps break down our invisible walls? I've since wondered if we would have been as willing to sing if the lights had been on inside the coach. Somehow, I think not. I believe we often show our real selves when no one can see us. We're more childlike when the lights are out and we can act how old we feel rather than how old we look.

I've always wondered how old I'd be if I didn't know how old I am. I suppose I'd be a young teenager, singing as if I were at camp in Yellowstone National Park. It's nice to know my wife and our new friends would probably answer the same. Perhaps we should turn out the lights more often. We might enjoy life more.

JUST NOTES

"It is better to light one small candle than to curse the darkness."

Confucius

28

The Leader

His hand touched mine just as I was reaching for a cup of punch. I was enjoying presenting a quality seminar on a university campus for a large manufacturer. All 35 attendees were executives who'd been around the block a few times. Well travelled, well read, and used to getting their way—you know the type. Good people, but very focused on work only. At least, that's what I thought.

The gentleman who touched my hand was tan and balding, and I shall never forget him. In his late 50s, he had kind eyes, and was handsome, well-groomed, and quiet. He asked if he could speak with me alone for a moment. "Surely," I said, and we walked over to a large, roaring fire in a beautiful fireplace I like to think was built especially for our seminar.

He said, "You're a fine speaker, Mr. Black, and I've heard a lot of speakers and attended a lot of seminars in my time."

I tried to be modestly polite and get away with a simple "Thank you, sir, I appreciate that." Realizing he wanted much more, I watched as he pulled out his wallet and began searching through it for something. Finally, he pulled out a picture of a beautiful young lady in a prom dress.

"This was my daughter. She died of cancer when she was eighteen. I wish you could have known her. She would have liked you, Joe."

He continued, "Yesterday, you described a leader as anyone who chooses to set a positive example for others to follow. You pointed out that each of us must decide every day whether we are going to respond positively or negatively to the realities we face. You're so right," he went on. "My Carolyn was a leader; she was until the day she died. So thank you, Joe, for reminding me of that fact. I'm so glad our paths crossed."

With tears in his eyes, he shook my hand and walked away. As I turned to the fireplace, I composed myself, wiped my eyes, and said a silent prayer of thanks for having met yet another wonderful human being. I turned and walked back into the corporate world, ready to talk about the cost of errors and measurement. I looked out at the president of the company. I wondered if he knew how fortunate he was to have as an associate the man who had just touched my hand and my heart.

Later in the seminar I made the point that true leaders look not only at tasks to be accomplished, but also at the care and love ratios which we have for one another. The group was deeply touched. I hadn't planned to do this—it just happened, thanks to my friend sharing a secret part of himself with me. It proved to be a great seminar with that company, all because of a leader named Carolyn and her loving father.

JUST NOTES

_____

_____

_____

_____

_____

_____

"Example is not the main thing in influencing others. It is the only thing."

Albert Schweitzer

_____

_____

_____

_____

_____

_____

_____

_____

_____

_____

_____

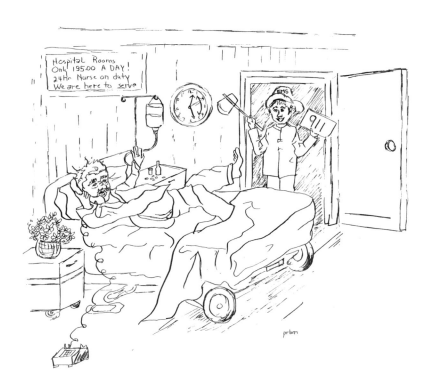

29

Third Shift on a Bedpan

You think you're short-handed at work? Well, listen to this. About midnight, an elderly man rang the nurse from his hospital bed, explaining he needed to relieve himself. The nurse helped the old fellow onto his bedpan and left. She assured him when he finished, he could buzz her and she'd return to remove the pan and help him get back to sleep.

After a few minutes, the old gentleman rang the bell and waited. Five minutes passed and no nurse. He rang and rang until finally, after 50 minutes still sitting on the bedpan, he decided to go nuclear. He picked up the phone and dialed 911! He explained to the Emergency Medical Service that he was stranded on a bedpan, miserable, and no one would come to help him. Well, the emergency crew came to his room, removed him from the bedpan, and helped clean him up. A bevy of nurses followed.

This is a true story! The hospital doesn't want it told for obvious reasons. I think, however, it's a great story that needs to be told about health care and customer service in some hospitals. Old and young alike, in or out of the medical field, should call 911 when they're not treated as paying customers should be. The next time you're left "sitting on a bedpan," may I suggest that you, too, dial 911 and watch 'em come a-running!

JUST NOTES

"God helps those who persevere."

Unknown

30

What? Me Retire?

The word retire–what does it mean to you? Apparently, it has many different meanings for a lot of people. Recently I mentioned to someone that I was 44 years old and that when I reached 50, I hoped my wife and I would have several alternative lifestyles to choose from. The gentleman then said, "Fifty is too young to retire!"

Retire? Who said anything about retiring? I simply said, "Alternative lifestyles."

To me, retiring means replanning and doing! It doesn't mean quitting!

Are there things you really want to do in life but haven't had the time? Would you like to take a less-travelled highway and perhaps occasionally enjoy a country lane? Would you like to have freedom to slow down (not stop) and smell the roses? I would, and I hope that time will come sooner than later.

To me, retiring means:

Redirecting our

Energy

Towards

Interests which

Really are

Important to

Nurture our personal

Growth and that of others we value and love.

Retiring often spawns new careers. More often than not the people I know who have retired haven't retired in the traditional sense. Instead, they've gone on to be very active, and more importantly, give a great deal of their time helping others in various ways.

So...retire? Absolutely, but never quit! Just think—you probably have your most exciting and meaningful years ahead of you. The opportunity to add value to your life and the lives of others is there. Let me challenge you to take the opportunity. Don't retire. Replan!

"*A person grows old with the hardening of ideas, not the arteries.*"

Unknown

31

Making a Difference

Are you ready to make a difference instead of just making a living? It's easy to make a buck, but it's hard to make a difference. The great news is that we can do both! You may well be doing both already. If you're not, let me challenge you to do so.

Each of us has unique talents. The world needs people who will dedicate themselves to becoming real leaders–people who have attitudes worth catching!

I assure you each person reading these words is a role model for someone somewhere. Somebody is looking to you to set an example, to lead the way, to listen, and to care. Be somebody who makes a difference to someone else. Don't be just another business person, another friend, husband, wife, parent–another person just going through the motions in life. Be somebody special by helping others achieve their hopes and dreams.

Each of us has the opportunity daily to accept this challenge. The United States and indeed the world have never needed leaders more than today. Real leaders are those willing to do the right things for the right reasons. Our individual and collective challenge must be to define and accept this responsibility–to change our behavior and execute our plan. We should accept this opportunity to lead, not only for ourselves but also for countless millions who will follow in our footsteps in the 21st century. We can leave a legacy of leadership if we choose. But no one else can do it for us.

As you lead, carefully consider not only the return on your investment (ROI) but also the return of integrity (ROI). We must invest in both if we're to truly make a difference that will result in a better future for those who follow. Look over your shoulder; someone is watching you. Make a difference.

JUST NOTES

_____

_____

_____

_____

_____

_____

"The biggest mistake you can make is to believe you are working for someone else."

W. Clement Stone

_____

_____

_____

_____

_____

_____

_____

_____

_____

_____

_____

_____

Stay in Touch!

Call me . . . Fax me . . . Write me . . .

Joe Black
Executive Quality Management, Inc.
205 E. Henry St.
Spartanburg, SC 29304
Fax: 803-573-6085

PHONE: 803-573-5234

Give the Gift of Quality to Your Colleagues and Friends!

ORDER FORM

YES, I want ___ copies of *The Attitude Connection: Focus on Quality* at $14.95 each, plus $2 shipping per book. (South Carolina residents please include 75¢ state sales tax.) Canadian orders must be accompanied by a postal money order in US funds. Allow 30 days for delivery.

___ Check/money order enclosed
Charge my: ___ VISA ___ MasterCard

Name _____

Phone (_____) _____

Address _____

City/State/Zip _____

Card # _____ Expires _____

Signature _____

Check your leading bookstore
Or call your credit card order to: 1-800-348-9953

Please make your check payable and return to:

Life Vision Books
P.O. Box 98
Campobello, SC 29322